Global Warming

Chris Oxlade

Bridgestone Books
an imprint of Capstone Press
Mankato, Minnesota

Originally published as Global Warming, ©2002 Franklin Watts, United Kingdom

Bridgestone Books are published by Capstone Press
151 Good Counsel Drive, P.O. Box 669, Mankato, MN 56002
http://www.capstone-press.com

Library of Congress Cataloging-in-Publication Data

Oxlade, Chris.
  Global warming / by Chris Oxlade.
      v. cm. -- (Our planet in peril)
Includes bibliographical references and index.
Contents: About global warming -- The atmosphere and the weather -- The
greenhouse effect -- Greenhouse gases -- Upsetting the balance --
Gathering evidence -- Changing climates -- More causes of climate change
-- Modeling the future -- Effects of global warming -- Problems for us
-- Stopping global warming -- Waking up to global warming.
  ISBN 0-7368-1361-6 (hardcover)
 1. Global warming--Juvenile literature. 2. Greenhouse gases--Juvenile
literature. 3. Climatic changes--Juvenile literature. [1. Global
warming. 2. Greenhouse gases. 3. Climatic changes.] I. Title. II.
Series.
  QC981.8.G56 O98 2003
  363.738'74--dc21

                                        2002009823

Editor: Kate Banham   Illustration: Ian Thompson
Designer: Mark Mills   Picture Research: Diana Morris
Art Direction: Jonathan Hair   Consultant: Sally Morgan, Ecoscene

Acknowledgements

The publishers would like to thank the following for permission to reproduce
photographs in this book.

Toshiyuki Aizawal/Reuters/Popperfoto: 29t; Jim Amos/SPL: 16t; Klaus Andrews/Still
Pictures: 4tr, 15bl; Alex Bartel/Ecoscene: 26t; Alian Compost/Still Pictures: 8t; Anthony
Cooper/Ecoscene: 21b, 27bl; DERA/Still Pictures: 7cl; Digital Vision: front cover, 10-11b,
16b, 23c, 25t, 28b; Index Stock/Zephyr Picture: 12; PhotoDisc: 4bl; Ecoscene: 11t; Mark
Edwards/Still Pictures: 13c; DOE/NREL/Warren Gretz: 27br; Chris Fairclough: 5b, 15cr;
FEMA News Photo/Saville: 22b; Pierre Gleizes/Still Pictures: 21t; Richard
Glover/Ecoscene: 7b, 11b; Skjold Photographs: 23b; Andy Hibbert/Ecoscene: 16b; David
Hoffman/Environmental Picture Library: 19t; FEMA News Photo: 5c; Harvey
Lloyd/Still Pictures: 24-25b; Vanessa Miles/Environmental Images: 13b; Hank
Morgan/SPL: 14b, 20c; NASA/SPL: 9t, 23t; Novosti/SPL: 17t; Popperfoto: 29t, 29b;
John Sanford/SPL: 19b; Kevin Schafer/Still Pictures: 27t; Francois Suchel/Still Pictures:
8b; Alan Towse/Ecoscene: 14t; NOAA/Bill Koch: 15t; Albert Visage/Still Pictures: 24t.

Contents

Words printed in *italics* are explained in the glossary.

Storms, dry periods, coastal flooding, food shortages, and habitat destruction are signs of *global warming*. Scientists warn that the planet will be in increasing danger in the coming years from these natural disasters if global warming is not reduced.

What is global warming?

Global warming is an increase in the temperature of the Earth's *atmosphere*. Weather records show that during the 20th century, the atmosphere warmed by less than one degree. Scientists predict, or expect, this warming to continue. They think global warming is caused mainly by gases produced when people burn coal, oil, and other *fossil fuels*. The gases trap the Sun's heat in our atmosphere. One of these gases is *carbon dioxide*.

Industry pours a huge amount of carbon dioxide into the atmosphere.

The growth of orange trees may be affected by global warming someday.

Climate change

You might think that a slightly warmer atmosphere would not be a problem. In fact, in colder countries, it could be an advantage. But the main effect of global warming will be a change in the world's weather, with some terrible effects. The Earth's annual weather patterns, climates, will change. This effect is known as *climate change*.

In 50 years

If global warming continues, what will the world be like in 50 years' time? *Climatologists*, scientists who study climates, think the atmosphere will warm by at least another degree. Patterns of sunshine, rainfall, and storms will change. Climate changes will change how plants and crops grow, affecting our food supplies. The sea level will also rise, leading to more flooding along low-lying coasts.

It is not too late

Most scientists agree global warming is happening and is caused by activities on Earth. They also agree global warming can be stopped and even reduced over the next few years if the amount of gases put into the atmosphere is reduced.

One of the expected effects of global warming is an increase in rainfall in some areas. This increase may cause floods.

◆ How you can help

Car engines burn gasoline or diesel fuel and are one of the main producers of the gases that cause global warming. A simple way to help reduce global warming is to walk or ride a bicycle.

If you can walk or bike to school, you can help reduce global warming.

Global warming happens in the Earth's atmosphere. The atmosphere is like a blanket of air that surrounds the Earth. Air is constantly swirling around the atmosphere, and this swirling creates the weather.

Atmospheric layers

Compared to the size of the Earth, the atmosphere is very shallow. Instead of a definite end, it gradually gets thinner until it fades into space, about 185 miles (300 kilometers) above the Earth's surface. Meteorologists, or scientists who study the atmosphere, divide the atmosphere into several layers. Weather happens in the lowest level of the atmosphere, called the troposphere.

Gases in the air

The air in the atmosphere is a mixture of many different gases. It is about 79 percent nitrogen and 20 percent oxygen. The remaining percentage is made up mainly of a gas called argon. Carbon dioxide makes up about 0.035 percent of the air. The air also contains water vapor, or water in gas form.

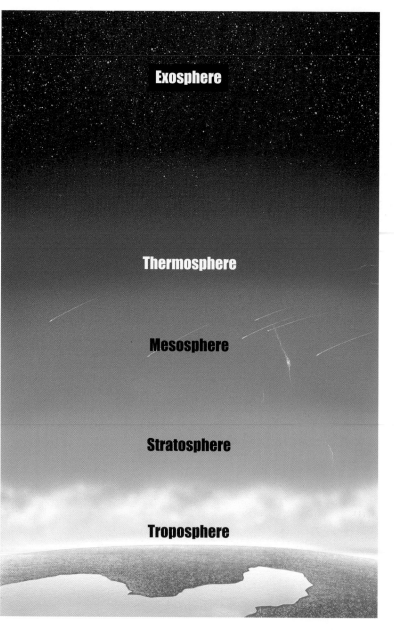

Exosphere

Thermosphere

Mesosphere

Stratosphere

Troposphere

The layers of the Earth's atmosphere.

Driving the weather

All the energy that drives the world's weather comes from the Sun. But the Sun's energy heats different parts of the Earth's surface in different ways. Near the equator, the tropics are warmer than the poles. The land heats up and cools down more quickly than the oceans, but the oceans store heat for much longer than the land. The land and oceans heat the air above them, making the air in some parts of the atmosphere warmer than in other parts. This uneven heating causes the air to swirl, creating winds.

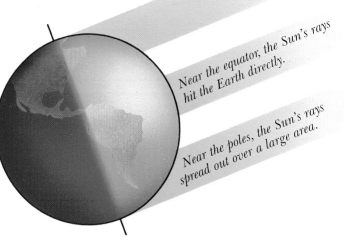

Near the equator, the Sun's rays hit the Earth directly.

Near the poles, the Sun's rays spread out over a large area.

The Sun's rays spread out more the farther they are from the equator, so their heat is also spread out.

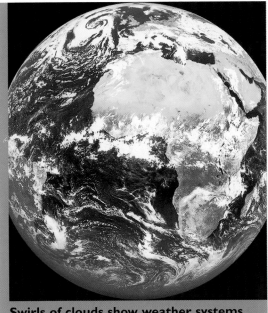

Swirls of clouds show weather systems caused by the uneven way in which the Sun heats the Earth.

Science in action

This experiment shows how snow, dark soil, and other types of land cover absorb different amounts of sunlight and have different effects on the air above. This absorbing is called the albedo effect.

You will need 2 pieces of tagboard, one white and one black.

Place both pieces of tag board in the sunshine. After a few minutes, feel both. Is one warmer than the other?

What is a climate?

Climate is the general pattern of weather that a place has over a long period of time. Although the weather in a particular place can change quite a lot from day to day, the climate stays the same from year to year. For example, a temperate climate has dry, warm summers and cool, wet winters, even though it can rain one day and be dry the next at any time of the year.

A tropical climate is hot all year, with heavy rain nearly every day.

The greenhouse effect

The Sun provides the heat that keeps the Earth warm.

When the Sun shines, a greenhouse gets warmer inside than out. This heating occurs because the greenhouse glass traps heat energy. Energy from the Sun goes through the glass, but heat from inside cannot escape. In a similar way, the Earth's atmosphere traps energy from the Sun. This is known as the *greenhouse effect*.

Energy in

The Sun gives off rays of energy called radiation. The radiation travels through space at the speed of light, 186,000 miles (300,000 kilometers) per second and reaches the Earth eight minutes later. Some of the radiation appears as light. The rest is made up of heat and ultraviolet light. Clouds reflect about one-third of the radiation back into space. Some is absorbed by the atmosphere, heating it slightly. The Earth's surface reflects some back into space. The rest is absorbed by the surface, raising temperatures.

Clouds reflect radiation into space. More cloud cover reduces the greenhouse effect.

Energy out

The warmed surface of the Earth emits energy back into the atmosphere in the form of heat energy called infrared radiation, not as light. The surface changes the energy from light to heat. Most of this infrared radiation escapes into space, but gases in the atmosphere known as *greenhouse gases* absorb some. This means that the atmosphere takes up the heat, making the atmosphere warmer.

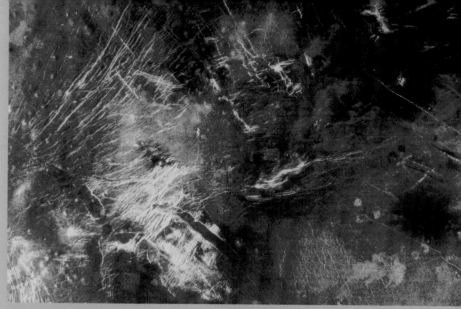

This radar image shows the surface of Venus. The surface temperature is 896°F (480°C).

Earth's atmosphere, containing greenhouse gases

heat from the Sun

Some heat is trapped in the Earth's atmosphere, instead of escaping into space.

Hot and cold

The greenhouse effect traps heat, and the swirling air in the atmosphere spreads the heat around the world. If there were no greenhouse effect, heat from the Earth's surface would escape straight into space without warming the atmosphere. The Earth would be much colder, almost covered in ice, and probably lifeless.

A natural balance

Some people believe only human activities cause the greenhouse effect. But it is a natural process that has been going on for billions of years. The greenhouse effect traps heat in the atmosphere, but only temporarily. Overall, the same amount of energy escapes as comes from the Sun. So the average temperature of the atmosphere stays the same.

◆ Science in action

Create a simple greenhouse model.

You will need a cardboard box, black paint or black paper, transparent plastic food wrap, pen, and thermometer.

Paint the inside of the cardboard box black (or line it with black paper). Cover the top with the plastic food wrap. With a pen, pierce a hole in the box's side. Stand the box outside in the sunshine. After half an hour, measure the temperature inside and outside the box.

Greenhouse gases

The gases that absorb heat in the atmosphere are known as greenhouse gases. They make up less than 0.1 percent of the atmosphere. Some greenhouse gases occur naturally, and some come from human activities.

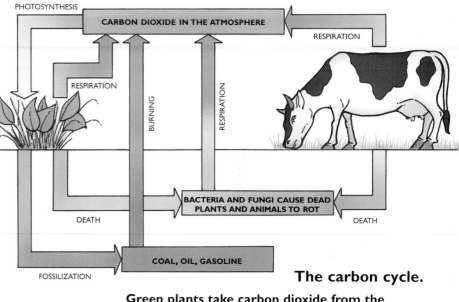

PHOTOSYNTHESIS

CARBON DIOXIDE IN THE ATMOSPHERE

RESPIRATION

RESPIRATION

BURNING

RESPIRATION

DEATH

BACTERIA AND FUNGI CAUSE DEAD PLANTS AND ANIMALS TO ROT

DEATH

FOSSILIZATION

COAL, OIL, GASOLINE

The carbon cycle.

Green plants take carbon dioxide from the atmosphere, and animal *respiration* and the rotting of dead matter return it.

Carbon dioxide

Carbon dioxide is one of the main greenhouse gases. It is made up of the chemical elements carbon and oxygen. Carbon dioxide makes up about 0.035 percent of the atmosphere. This percentage is often written down as 350 parts per million (*ppm*), meaning there are 350 carbon dioxide molecules in every million molecules of gas in the air.

The carbon cycle

All the complex chemicals that make up plants, animals, and other organisms contain strings of carbon atoms. Carbon is constantly moving between animals and plants, the land and oceans, and the atmosphere, where it is contained in carbon dioxide. As part of the carbon cycle, carbon dioxide constantly enters and leaves the atmosphere.

Rain forests take in and give out more carbon dioxide than any other *ecosystem*.

How carbon moves around

Plants and animals emit carbon dioxide when they respire. Plants also take in carbon dioxide when they produce food by photosynthesis. When plants and animals die, bacteria, fungi, and other *decomposers* break down their parts. The decomposers release carbon dioxide into the air. The oceans take in and give off carbon dioxide.

More greenhouse gases

Water vapor, which enters the atmosphere when water *evaporates* from soil, plants, and oceans, is the gas that is most responsible for the natural greenhouse effect. *Ozone*, a form of oxygen that occurs at some levels of the atmosphere, is another greenhouse gas. The other natural greenhouse gases are methane and nitrous oxide. Termites, cattle, and other animals produce methane. It also comes from swamps. Nitrous oxide comes from rotting vegetation.

The carbon that came from the atmosphere when this tree grew returns to the atmosphere as the tree rots.

◆ Sustainable solution

Reforestation in Kaingaroa Forest, New Zealand.

As plants grow, they take in carbon dioxide from the atmosphere to make food. The carbon from the carbon dioxide is used to build the substances that make up the plant. Planting new trees in places where forests have been cut down is called reforestation. It will help to remove excess carbon dioxide from the air.

Upsetting the balance

Every day, hundreds of millions of cars put carbon dioxide into the atmosphere.

Since the Industrial Revolution began in Europe in the mid-1700s, humans have been adding extra greenhouse gases to the atmosphere. This has upset the natural balance of greenhouse gases, creating an increase in the greenhouse effect. This increase causes global warming.

Carbon dioxide from fuels

We add huge amounts of carbon dioxide to the atmosphere by burning coal, gasoline, oil, and other fossil fuels in cars, factories, and power stations. Carbon dioxide is made when these fuels are burned. In the developed world, each person's energy use is responsible for putting about 11 tons (10 metric tons) of carbon dioxide into the atmosphere every year.

Carbon dioxide from forests

The cutting down, or deforestation, of the world's rain forests adds carbon dioxide to the atmosphere. When people clear the forest for farming or ranching, most of the vegetation is burned or rots. This burning or rotting releases carbon dioxide into the atmosphere. Normally, the forest cannot regrow, so new plants cannot take in the carbon dioxide.

Slash-and-burn farming destroys the fragile forest soil, preventing regrowth of the forest.

Carbon dioxide in the atmosphere

Oceans and plants soak up about one-third of the carbon dioxide that goes into the atmosphere because of human activities. The rest stays in the atmosphere. At the present rate, there will be more than 700 ppm of carbon dioxide in the atmosphere by 2100. That's double what it is now, and three times the level before the Industrial Revolution.

Old refrigerators contain **CFCs** that can be released when the refrigerator is thrown away.

Particles in the air

Not all the pollutants put into the atmosphere add to the greenhouse effect. Microscopic particles of solids and liquids created by burning fuels, by agriculture, and by industry actually reflect energy from the Sun, reducing the greenhouse effect.

Sources of other gases

The amount of methane in the atmosphere more than doubled in the 20th century, mainly because of cattle ranching and rice growing. These activities create methane. Nitrous oxide also has increased because of agriculture and chemical industries. Gases called *chlorofluorocarbons* (*CFCs*) have also been added. Spray cans, refrigerators, and air conditioners once widely used CFCs. They add to the greenhouse effect. Sulfur dioxide and other polluting gases react chemically with the air to produce more ozone in the lower atmosphere.

◆ How you can help

Every time you boil water in a kettle or turn on a light, you are using electricity that has probably been produced by burning fossil fuels in power stations. If you only boil as much water as you need and turn lights off when not using them, less carbon dioxide will go into the atmosphere. You also can buy energy-efficient lightbulbs that use only a fraction of the energy ordinary lightbulbs use.

Energy-efficient lightbulbs help to reduce global warming.

Gathering evidence

The news media, newspapers, and books provide facts and figures about the greenhouse effect, global warming, and climate change today. It is also important to know what the climate was like 10 years ago, 100 years ago, and even millions of years ago.

Measuring the weather

Every day, *meteorological* organizations in every country of the world monitor the weather. The organizations measure temperature, rainfall, wind speed and direction, air pressure, sunshine, and the type and number of clouds. Meteorologists use the data to produce weather forecasts. The data is also stored as a record of the past weather and used to investigate possible climate change.

An automatic weather station powered by solar cells.

Computers are perfect machines for storing the huge amount of weather data collected every day.

Climate clues

More than just the weather provides evidence for global warming and climate change. Climatologists make many other observations and measurements, often using data from remote-sensing satellites. For example, climatologists record ocean temperatures and currents, the area of snow cover, the extent of sea ice at the poles, the length of glaciers, and changing vegetation patterns.

The snow from a March 1966 blizzard nearly buried utility poles in Jamestown, North Dakota.

Weather records

Vast amounts of data from thousands of weather stations are stored every day to create weather records. Accurate weather records are available only for the years since 1861, when organized recording began. But historical documents provide an idea of what climates were like before that.

The distant past

To learn about climates thousands or millions of years ago, scientists look at fossils. Fossils tell what sort of animals and plants lived in a certain place or time. By comparing where similar animals and plants live today, scientists can understand what the climate was like.

Analyzing bubbles of gas in deep polar ice shows what the atmosphere was like thousands of years ago.

◆ Science in action

Nature is often a good guide to how climate has changed. Trees grow better in warmer, sunnier years than in colder, cloudier years. Try measuring the tree rings of a cut log. There is a ring for each year of growth. Wider rings show more growth in that year, indicating that the weather was warmer.

Changing climates

One of the main effects of global warming is climates around the world are beginning to change slightly. But changing climates are not a new thing.

When this dinosaur died, the world's overall temperature was far warmer than today.

Temperature changes

The Earth has experienced many cycles of warming and cooling since it formed more than 4 billion years ago. For example, 100 million years ago during the *Cretaceous* period, the *average global temperature* was about 18°F (8°C) higher than it is today. Dinosaurs lived in forests at the South Pole, and a warm tropical sea covered much of today's land.

Today, only animals such as penguins and seals live at the South Pole. At one time, the South Pole was home to forests and dinosaurs.

Periods of cold

Ice ages were periods up to 100,000 years long when the average global temperature was a few degrees lower than it is today. The ice caps that today cover the poles extended over northern Europe, North America, South America, and Australia. The last ice age ended about 10,000 years ago. It is possible another ice age might occur in the next few thousand years.

Mammoths found in frozen ground lived during the last ice age.

Recent climate change

Weather records show that global warming is happening. The average global temperature of about 60°F (15°C) increased less than one degree during the 20th century. Overall, the 1990s were the warmest decade since weather records were started, and 1998 was the warmest year ever.

More evidence for global warming

A study of photographs taken from satellites shows that snow cover across the world has reduced by about 10 percent since the 1960s. Glaciers in the world's high mountain ranges are shrinking by a few miles or kilometers a year. Since the 1950s, Arctic sea ice has reduced about 10 percent. In 1995, an iceberg about 22 miles (35 kilometers) wide, 47 miles (76 kilometers) long, and 220 yards (200 meters) thick broke off from Antarctica. Sea levels rose between 4 and 10 inches (10 and 25 centimeters) in the 20th century.

This chart shows how the average global temperature has changed over the last 100 years.

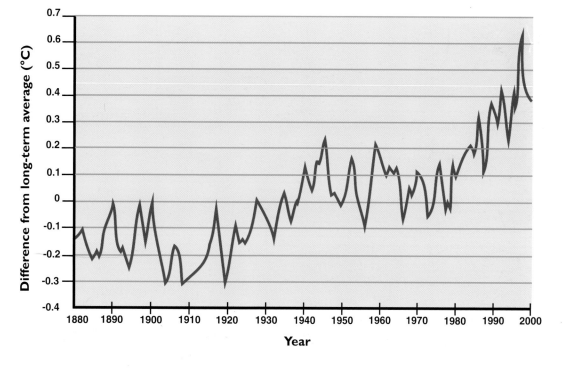

Difference from long-term average (°C)

Year

Most scientists agree that climates around the world appear to be changing. But the greenhouse effect and global warming are not necessarily the cause of all climate changes. Other factors can affect the climate.

warm water evaporates, producing storm clouds

warm surface waters are pushed east instead of west

Australia   Pacific Ocean   South America

El Niño

El Niño (pronounced "el-NEEN-yoh") is a natural event that happens every few years. During an El Niño event, which lasts about 12–18 months, the currents in the Pacific Ocean near South America change direction, bringing warmer-than-normal water to the ocean's surface. This affects the climate locally and globally. Scientists believe the 1997–1998 El Niño caused storms and floods in Peru, crop failures in East Africa, forest fires in Indonesia, and thousands of deaths worldwide. Climatologists do not understand how or why El Niño happens.

Catastrophes

Volcanic eruptions and meteor impacts may cause climate change by sending large amounts of dust into the atmosphere. When Mount Pinatubo in the Philippines erupted in 1991, a vast cloud of ash and droplets of acid rose 25 miles (40 kilometers) into the atmosphere and spread slowly around the world. This cloud reflected some of the Sun's energy into space. Global temperatures dropped by less than one degree for more than a year.

The impact of a huge meteor would throw enough dust into the atmosphere to reduce global temperatures for years.

Logging destroys large areas of rain forest, causing local climate change.

Changing land use

Human activities on the land can also change the climate. Changing the amount of vegetation changes how much energy the land reflects and absorbs. This change can affect the temperature, cloud formation, and rainfall. For example, scientists think cutting down the rain forests will reduce the amount of water vapor that goes back into the air from the forests, reducing the amount of rainfall.

Space cycles

Some scientists think cycles in the movement of the Earth and the Sun's activity cause long-term climate changes. One theory is that a slight wobble in the Earth over thousands of years changes how heat spreads over the surface and causes ice ages.

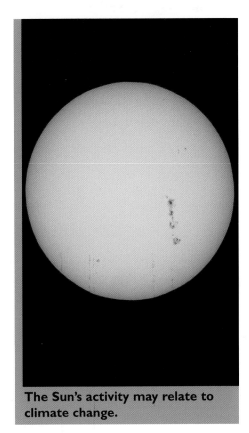

The Sun's activity may relate to climate change.

Modeling the future

Research shows what has happened to the climate in the past. Scientists frequently try to predict future climates. Climatologists make these predictions in many ways.

This researcher is testing a model to predict climate changes caused by the greenhouse effect.

Computer models

The way the greenhouse effect works, how it creates global warming, and how climates are affected is complicated. To predict the future, climatologists use complex computer programs called general circulation models (GCMs). They are mathematical models of the atmosphere. Even on powerful supercomputers, the programs take hours or even days to come up with an answer.

How hot could it get?

Climatologists give *climate models* data about how much of each greenhouse gas will probably enter the atmosphere every year. Computer programs predict what climates will be like as far as 100 years in the future. The latest models predict that the global average temperature at the Earth's surface will rise between 2.7 and 10.8°F (1.5 and 5.8°C) by 2100.

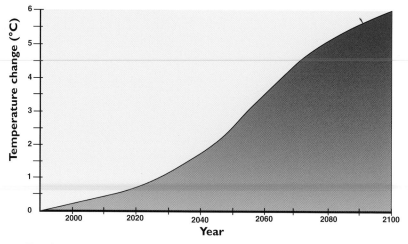

During the 21st century, the Earth's average temperature could rise by 5.8°C.

Model problems

Computer climate models can only do the calculations that climatologists program them to do. If the atmosphere works in a slightly different way from what scientists think it will, the models will give the wrong answers. For example, climatologists do not completely understand the effect clouds have on global warming, or exactly how much carbon dioxide the oceans soak up.

Different views

Various people and organizations hold different views on the seriousness of global warming. Organizations such as oil companies often say that climatologists have not proved a link between human activities and global warming. Environmental organizations often quote the worst-case scenario predicted by climatologists.

◆ How you can help

People who feel strongly about reducing global warming often support Greenpeace, Friends of the Earth, or other environmental campaign groups. Web addresses for these groups are on page 30.

Oil companies tend to downplay the effects of global warming.

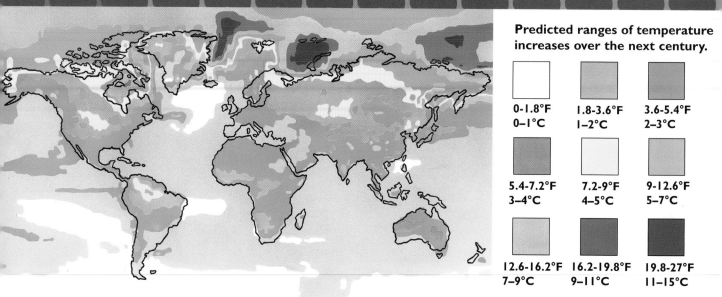

Predicted ranges of temperature increases over the next century.

0-1.8°F 0-1°C	1.8-3.6°F 1-2°C	3.6-5.4°F 2-3°C
5.4-7.2°F 3-4°C	7.2-9°F 4-5°C	9-12.6°F 5-7°C
12.6-16.2°F 7-9°C	16.2-19.8°F 9-11°C	19.8-27°F 11-15°C

If the average global temperature rises by about 5°F (3°C) by the end of this century, what do climatologists predict will happen to climates? Global warming will probably affect daily temperatures around the world, change the pattern of rainfall, and increase the severity of storms.

Drier and wetter

Climate models predict global warming will cause about 5 percent more rainfall by 2100. But that does not mean everywhere will be wetter. North America, northern Europe, and northern Asia will get more rain, but countries in the tropics will get less. Changing rainfall patterns mean rivers will flood more often in winter in some places, but other places could have drought.

Hotter and colder

Computer climate models predict an average rise in global temperatures of about 5°F (3°C). The temperature will not rise by this amount all over the world. In the world's higher *latitudes*, nearer the poles, the increase may be 9°F or 10°F (5°C or 6°C). Overall, this would mean more very hot days and fewer very cold days.

In 1997, East Grand Forks, Minnesota, had a major river flood due to increased precipitation.

Storms on the way

Winter storms and hurricanes get their energy from the warm oceans. As sea temperatures rise, these storms will be able to gather more energy. Winds will be stronger and carry more rain. This will lead to increased damage from high winds and flooding both inland and on the coast from *storm surges*.

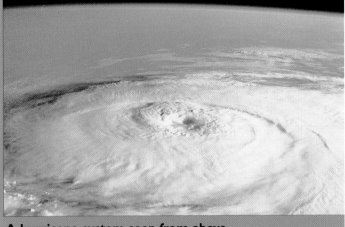

A hurricane system seen from above.

Vegetation will have difficulty surviving in areas that already receive little rainfall.

Deserts and forests

Climate change will affect how natural vegetation grows around the world. By about 2050, large areas of rain forests and tropical grasslands may turn to dusty deserts because of less rain and rising temperatures. But in the Northern Hemisphere, forests will actually grow larger because there will be more rain, higher temperatures, and more carbon dioxide in the atmosphere. One advantage is that these forests will take in some of the carbon dioxide in the atmosphere.

How you can help

Recycling is a good way of helping cut down global warming. Recycling saves not only the materials the goods are made from, but also the energy that would be needed to make new materials. Using energy means burning fossil fuels.

Always try to recycle plastic bottles, glass, tins, and paper.

Problems for us

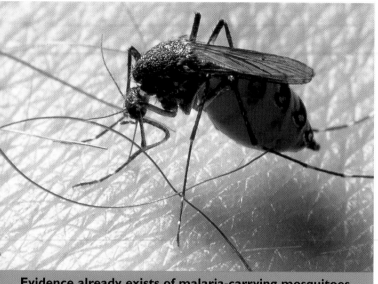

Evidence already exists of malaria-carrying mosquitoes spreading to new habitats as climates begin to change.

Global warming will create climate changes. But a change in the weather is a minor problem compared to other problems that global warming and climate change might cause. Humans, animals, and plants would all suffer.

Water resources

Changing rainfall patterns means many countries will have less water for drinking and watering crops. Unfortunately, most of these countries are already short of water. By the end of the century, 100 million more people could be short of water. To make matters worse, if the world's population continues to increase, more people will have to share a smaller amount of water.

Food for thought

Changing temperatures and rainfall patterns will affect how well crops grow. In the tropics, reduced rainfall will reduce the amount of food that can be grown. Farther north and south, warmer climates will increase how much food can be grown. But overall, production of important crops such as wheat will fall, leading to increased food prices. In some countries, millions of people will be hungry.

Reduced rainfall as a result of global warming will reduce yields of wheat and other important crops.

Rising sea levels

Climate models predict a rise in sea levels of about 2 feet (61 centimeters) by the end of the century. That does not sound like much, but it would put 200 million people living near coasts under threat of flooding, especially in stormy areas. Melting ice from ice caps flowing into the oceans will cause the rise in sea level. Also, the water in the oceans will expand as it warms. In the distant future, if all the ice in the world melted, sea levels could rise by 71 yards (65 meters).

Low-lying coastal areas may be flooded so often that they will become uninhabitable.

◆ Science in action

Try this simple experiment to see how water expands as it warms.

You will need a plastic bottle, modeling clay, a transparent straw, a marker pen, and a bowl.

Fill the bottle to the brim with cold water. Mold a blob of modeling clay around the straw. Push the clay into the neck of the bottle to make a seal. Mark the height of the water in the straw. Stand the bottle in a bowl of warm water and watch the water expand up the straw.

Stopping global warming

In most countries, using more electricity means burning more coal, oil, or gasoline and creating more carbon dioxide.

At the beginning of the 21st century, carbon dioxide in the air continues to increase. Can global warming be stopped or reduced?

Cutting carbon emissions

The most important action to stop global warming is reducing carbon dioxide *emissions*. Most carbon dioxide emissions come from burning coal, oil, gasoline, and other fossil fuels in power stations. To stop carbon dioxide levels from rising above 360 ppm and prevent global warming from getting worse, emissions must be reduced by 60 percent. This is not practical at the moment, but people need to use electricity and fossil fuels more efficiently to burn less fuel. If carbon dioxide continues to enter the atmosphere at the present rate, there will be more than 700 ppm of carbon dioxide in the atmosphere by 2100.

Renewable energy

One way to use less fossil fuel in power stations is to make electricity in other ways. Renewable energy sources, such as solar power, wind power, *hydroelectric power,* and *tidal power* use energy that originally came from the Sun. In fact, the amount of energy that comes from the Sun is 6,000 times greater than the energy actually used.

Adapting to change

If climates do change as much as climatologists predict, people must act to prevent damage to property and people from the increased storms and floods. For example, extra *flood barriers* must be built, or people must move away from low-lying coasts. People in developing countries may need assistance to grow enough food.

Wind farms produce emission-free electricity, but some people consider wind farms ugly or noisy.

The Thames Barrier protects low-lying districts of London, England, from tidal surges. The barrier will have to be used more frequently if sea levels rise.

◆ Sustainable solution

One form of fuel that will help to reduce global warming is biomass fuel. It comes from burning plants or plant oils. The carbon dioxide that biomass fuels release when they burn is balanced by the carbon dioxide plants take in as they grow.

A vehicle powered by biomass fuel.

Waking up to global warming

Svante Arrhenius (1859–1927) was the first scientist to predict global warming.

More than 100 years ago, Swedish scientist Svante Arrhenius first introduced the idea of global warming and climate change. Arrhenius said the global temperature could rise by a few degrees because of the amount of coal and oil that was being burned. It was not until the 1980s that scientists began taking the idea seriously.

International efforts

The summer of 1988 in the United States was extremely hot. Wildfires caused millions of dollars of damage, and lack of rain resulted in poor grain production. These conditions helped persuade climatologists from many countries to form the Intergovernmental Panel of Climate Change (IPCC). The World Meteorological Organization supports the IPCC.

Frequent wildfires are a result of reduced rainfall.

Talking together

The first time the world's governments met to discuss global warming was at the 1992 Earth Summit, held in Rio de Janeiro, Brazil. Other conferences followed, including one in Kyoto, Japan, in 1997. Here, the Kyoto Protocol was suggested. This agreement says by 2012, countries should reduce carbon dioxide emissions to a level 5 percent below the emissions of 1990. In 2001, 180 countries agreed to the Kyoto Protocol.

Delegates from more than 100 countries attended the climate conference in Kyoto, Japan.

Difficult decisions

The United States has 5 percent of the world's population but produces 20 percent of the greenhouse gases. The United States did not agree to the Kyoto Protocol. The U.S. government is concerned that reducing emissions means loss of jobs and of freedom for people to use their cars. The cuts affect only the top-ranking industrialized countries. Even China and Russia do not have to follow the protocol. This accounts for some U.S. reluctance to make changes when competing nations are excluded.

In 2001, U.S. President George W. Bush suggested alternatives to the Kyoto Protocol.

Further information

These are websites you can use to learn more about topics mentioned in this book.

The Meteorological Office in Bracknell, UK, is the national weather service of the UK. The website at **www.met-office.gov.uk** offers forecasts and general weather information.

www.royal-met-soc.org.uk is the website of the Royal Meteorological Society, an organization for weather experts and other interested people.

For the latest news on climate change, visit the website of the World Meteorological Organization at **www.wmo.ch**. Details of the Intergovernmental Panel on Climate Change (IPCC) are also included.

The National Oceanic and Atmospheric Administration (NOAA) is the national weather forecasting service of the United States. Visit the website at **www.nws.noaa.gov** for forecasts and maps, which you can download.

For general environmental information, check out Friends of the Earth, an organization that campaigns worldwide to protect the environment. The website is at **www.foe.co.uk**.

You can also visit the Greenpeace website at **www.greenpeaceusa.org** for environmental information.

Glossary

Atmosphere
The layer of air that covers the Earth like a blanket.

Average global temperature
The average temperature of the atmosphere worldwide.

Carbon dioxide
A gas made of carbon and oxygen. It is the most important greenhouse gas.

Chlorofluorocarbon (CFC)
A chemical that destroys ozone in the atmosphere.

Climate change
A gradual change in the world's climate over time.

Climate model
A complicated computer program that predicts what will happen to the world's climate over many years.

Climatologist
A scientist who studies climates, climate change, and global warming.

Cretaceous
The period in geological time that lasted from 145 million years ago to 65 million years ago.

Decomposer
Something that breaks down dead matter into simpler chemicals.

Emission
A chemical given off by engines or power stations.

Evaporate
To change from a liquid to a gas.

Flood barrier
A damlike structure that prevents water from flowing inland along a river.

Fossil fuel
Fuel formed from the remains of animals and plants that died millions of years ago.

Global warming
A gradual increase in the average global temperature of the Earth's atmosphere.

Greenhouse effect
The way the Earth's atmosphere traps the Sun's heat.

Greenhouse gas
One of several gases that trap heat and that are responsible for the greenhouse effect.

Hydroelectric power
Electricity made using the energy in flowing water.

Latitude
The distance north or south of the equator, measured in degrees.

Meteorological
Dealing with the study of climates.

Ozone
A form of oxygen that occurs at some levels of the atmosphere.

ppm
Short for parts per million.

Respiration
The chemical processes in a cell that use oxygen and release carbon dioxide and energy.

Storm surge
An increase in sea level under an area of low pressure in the atmosphere, such as a hurricane.

Tidal power
Electricity made from the energy in rising and falling tides.

Index